ATTENTION DEFICIT DISORDER

The FOCUS PROGRAM
to improve the attention

Practical exercises
for school and home

Level I. Children from 3 to 7 years

by
Juan José Ibáñez Solar

INDEX

A Javi

4

1. The attention

Attention is a basic psychological function, and also a behavior. It is not only something internal but also something that is seen. We can observe when someone is distracted or when he is concentrated. The attention is that the child or the subject, focuses on certain aspects of the reality, of an object, of a problem or of an information (considered relevant or important) discarding others (considered secondary or can be dispensed with) Somehow, attention is like a filter that lets pass some data or stimuli, and not others. For this, the subject can follow a goal, an intention or not.

Attention, is a very important cognitive process because it allows us to learn, to advance or to survive. Our mind needs to limit the amount of information it has to process, because otherwise, it would be overtaken by a multitude of irrelevant data that would block us. It would be impossible to think, reason, choose, develop and finish a task, have a conversation or learn a language.

The attention has several aspects, for example:

1.- Amplitude: refers to the amount of data we can attend at once, or the number of activities we can do at the same time. For example, I can paint and listen to music simultaneously, but I may not be able to follow two different conversations without losing or finally neglecting one of them.

2.- Intensity and displacements: Attention can be "measured". Fluctuates

For example, when I am asleep, I have zero attention; When I am drowsy, my attention goes up to 1, 2 or 3. if I start to listen to the radio that starts to broadcast in the morning, my concentration level would be 4 or 5 points. While if I am studying a very interesting material in a quiet place, my ability to concentrate probably goes up to 7, 8 or 9. This same level occurs when I sing a song that I like a lot and enjoy singing it. I move my focus from one activity to another (the radio, the song, the study material...) that is, my attention is like a fluid passing from one object to another. And in each case, with different intensity.

That is, attention has different strength depending on various factors such as my internal state, the material that is offered as a stimulus, the environmental factors, my learning history or others. This intensity can vary, for example, if I am reading a book, it is possible that at some point it rests, or I may lose the reading thread, if I start to find myself tired or the text does not excite me. The attention has, therefore, oscillations during any activity.

Young children have more frequent attention lapses than young people or adults because their attention is a process that is being built and therefore has shorter periods of focus. This is well known by teachers of Early Childhood Education and therefore, the activities proposed in the classroom to children up to 6-7 years of age are usually short and above all, based on images or manipulative activities.

The drawings help to maintain the attention and this at any age, but especially in Early Childhood Education. The more complex a material, the more need we have to rely on images. In Spanish we say "an image, worth more than a thousand words".

This is also known by storytellers, who design beautiful drawings to be interspersed in written texts, so that the reader's attention becomes more focused.

Why do we say all this?

Because they are the principles on which we have based ourselves to design our program of improvement of the attention.

Let's recap:

1. For ages between 3 and 7 years. Improving care from an early age, prevention.
2. Practical activities, paper and pencil
3. Short Tasks.
4. Activities based on images.
5. With immediate reinforcement to build a good learning history in relation to care.
6. Dismissing the activity at times when the child is tired or does not have a good predisposition.

Attention is a flowing process, which has variations, ups and downs of intensity and even lapses or momentary losses. This is normal and obeys a defensive mechanism of the psychic apparatus, which stops, causing a' momentary disconnection. This happens to deal with the excess of information, the arrival of unwanted or uninteresting stimuli, and even to get away from sensations or painful information, internal or external.
In Spain, there is a very illustrative phrase to describe the moments when someone loses attention, it is said of him or her that "is in the moon of Valencia", or "is in the moon" simply.

When these episodes are numerous and substantially affect the work rhythm or performance and development of the child in various areas, we speak of "attention deficit".

3.- Control of care. It is necessary to differentiate between the basic psychological process that is the "attention" and the self-control or management of this mechanism that the subject does. The latter is called "meta-attention". It is the ability to handle one's attention. It is the ability to realize when I have attention and when not, to know why, and to be able to handle one's attention so that it turns on or disconnects in relation to a task.

For example, let's imagine that I am a student in Chemistry class. At some point I am distracted by a partner. If I become aware of my distraction and am able to re-activate my interest in the teacher's explanation, then I have developed a control of my attention, that is, a meta-attentional process. This capacity is acquiring with the years, being in the school stage when the attention has a greater development, whereas the meta-attentional processes must be firmly established in the secondary education. The meta-attention depends on processes of psychological maturation, motivational, emotional, but also with training, that is, with teaching, education, molding and our history of reinforcement.

En nuestro programa, también estimulamos la meta-atención, devolviendo al sujeto una ficha que hay que volver a repasar, porque hay algún error que ha pasado desapercibido al muchacho.

Factors of attention

Now, what does attention depend on? What factors influence it? This question has traditionally been answered with the same answer: there are two types of factors, internal and external factors. Let's go in parts, not ... lose attention:

External factors of attention.

1. The force of the Stimulus (E). We do not pay the same attention to the sound of a soft rain, that to the noise of a sudden ray. We do not put the same interest in a faded drawing, that another with well-defined outlines and colors and striking.

2. Changes. The changes in the stimuli always raise our attention. An example. I arrive home every day with my car the same way, I see the same gardens and houses. But it turns out that that day in the morning, the City Council has decided to place a small fountain on the sidewalk of my house. Arriving at noon of work, this change will draw my attention and I will focus on this (new) stimulus that that morning, when I left my home, it was not. Another example: if I am walking around the city and I see a group of people waiting for the bus, it may happen that the line is formed by ten subjects, but only one of them has glasses, or wear a hat, or is the only one wearing an umbrella . Well, it is likely to pay attention to this particular person, but not for nothing, but because it involves a change, from the rest of people who are there by his side.

3. The size. More attention is paid to a huge poster than to a small pamphlet stuck to the side. Ads in the newspaper are more expensive, if their size is larger.

4. Constancy or repetition of a stimulus. A little sign, may not make us pay attention. But if we continue walking around the city, and the same sign has been placed in many other places, it is probable that during our walk, we ended up saying "Well, to see, this poster! ... what does it say? I only see him everywhere! "

5. Movement. The change of place of an object is something to which we pay attention, especially if the environment remains fixed. Let's take a clear example. Imagine that we are in the army, and we are sergeants. We are in charge of a small group of men, a squad of twenty soldiers. They are standing, forming, firm, in front of us. All of them remain in a still situation since we are going to review. One of them, in the middle of the group, makes a gesture to look at his watch, its movement is minimal, but we catch it automatically, because all the soldiers around it are like statues. If the situation had been different, that same movement would not have attracted our attention, for example, if the movement of the components of the group had been allowed.

6. Contrast. It is very similar to some of the examples we have mentioned. It happens when a stimulus, is different from those around it. It is the one that catches our attention, but not because it is especially large, noisy or personally significant, but by comparison with the rest of environmental stimuli that surrounds it. In a field of white daisies, a red poppy, will be the stimulus that will capture us more safely.

Internal factors of attention.

1. Significance for the subject. For example, a mother who is sleeping is more sensitive to the baby's sobbing to wake up than another person or woman other than the mother. In this sense, the emotions of the individual and their affective relationship with the meaning of the stimulus play a singular importance.

2. Physical state. If I am hungry, I will probably be very sensitive to the smell of food, and less to other odors. My state of physiological need prepares me to pay special attention to certain kinds of stimuli.

3. Our interests, and values, make them as guides or filters that enable us to direct our attention to certain stimuli to the detriment of others. For example, if we are studying Chinese, it is easy for us to be more careful when we hear an accidental conversation in that idiom. When we want to cultivate our interests, we select some books from the thousands available in the library. This entails the ability to select things from all that the environment offers us. What interests us of attention is that it is a cognitive process, that has to do with the motivation itself, and that can be managed by the subject. In addition, it is something that can be stimulated, one can learn to be more attentive. It is not a process that is given to certain ages, but is part of our whole life, and remains with us until our death. For all this, attention is something that can be worked and improved, that is, we can become more effective in paying attention.

4. It is therefore a mental function that can be stimulated from early childhood education, from 3 or 4 years and even earlier. For this, it is essential to design and implement programs that enhance care in an organized way, so that the child becomes accustomed to paying attention to the relevant stimuli of a task. In this line, the program "Focus", includes a design of tasks adapted for the first ages and that based on images, can be used for this purpose.

2 ¿ How to work the activities?

General procedure

The activities are presented in tab format.

Each sheet has one sheet, independent of the next.

In each file, the child must do the same task:

A) identify (mark, round, underline) with a pencil, that drawing that is the same as the model, that is, it has the same orientation.

B) This order can be varied, for example: identify the object or objects, which are different from the model or oriented in different ways.

The more we intersperse these two orders, indicating one for some chips and the opposite for others, the more we will be hampering the work, and the more we will stimulate the mental flexibility in the subject.

For each token, the model drawing is always placed at the top of the sheet and separated from the rest of the stimuli by a thick black horizontal line. It is with this drawing of the upper zone, with which you have to compare the rest of the drawings of the sheet, that is, those that are under the horizontal line.

Raise the task as a game.

The activities must be done with pen, in case the subject must erase a wrong path.

Order of realization of the activities

It is recommended to start with the first page, since although the age of care improves, there are children of the same age who have very different competence in relation to the attentional processes.

Do not assume that a child has already a certain level, but it is recommended to work from the initial tab and move to the next when the boy has solved the card that occupies and corrected possible selection errors.

Generally, work is done first with concrete objects, then with signs and finally with letters. It also increases the number and complexity of the elements to be considered in each file. Sometimes we insert slightly more complex chips between those of a lower level, in order to observe the performance of the child.

Subjects to which the activities are directed

These exercises are designed for children between 3 and 7 years of age without difficulty. In this case, the "Focus" program is an activity with a preventive intention, that is, to improve the care of children from an early age.

It can also be used with older children who may have special educational needs or serious attention disorders. Likewise, the exercises can be used to work with children with attention deficit or who present difficulties of this type, especially in relation to "table work" or "school materials" such as tokens, etc.

Work environment

The child must work in a comfortable place, with adequate lighting and without being tired or unwilling to do so.

Restrict distracting objects during activities and do not let the next page pass until the adult (parent or teacher) has assessed the page that the boy has finished.

Evaluation and reinforcement.

The evaluation is a basic thing to improve the attention because when the child receives the message that he does the activities well, he builds a positive self-image (self-concept) in relation to the subject that concerns us: attention.

Therefore, the task is as important as proper self-reinforcement to the subject.

At the end of each sheet or sheet, properly, and even if you have identified errors, say to the child "Well, I see that you have paid attention" or "you are working paying attention to what you do" are the type of messages that the boy Needs to develop this positive self-concept in relation to the attentional. These reinforcements, we must not only give them when finishing each task, but also during the accomplishment of the same.

The complete completion of the program should be followed by a special prize, previously agreed with the child, taking into account the effort involved.

Failures

When in the assessment of the page, we detect that there is a failure, we will not tell the child what it is, but we will only provide information that   on that page that has just finished, there is a failure (or two, or three ...) And that he must find them before moving to the next page or ending that day.

Upper levels

To work with higher levels or ages, you can use the program "Focus" II (for children from 7 to 11 years) and "Focus" III (young people between 12 and 16 years)

"FOCUS"

PROGRAM TO IMPROVE THE ATTENTION

LEVEL I

CHILDREN from 3 to 7 years

<u>EXERCISES</u>

Identify drawings that are the same as the model

or

Identify drawings that are different from the model

Do the activities with paper and rubber

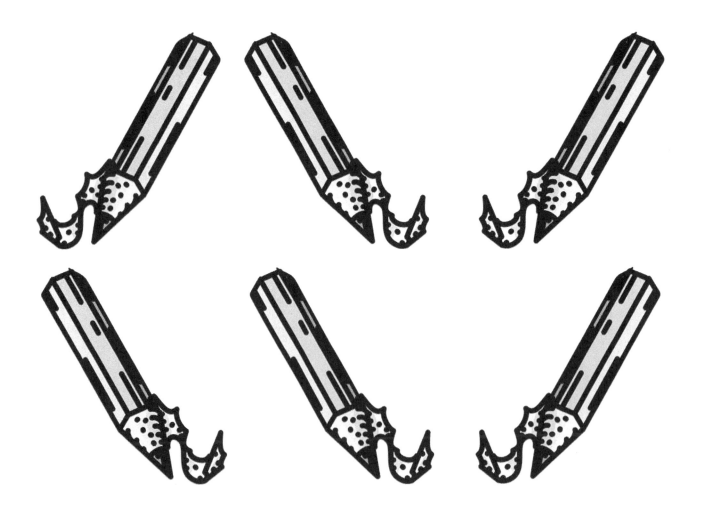

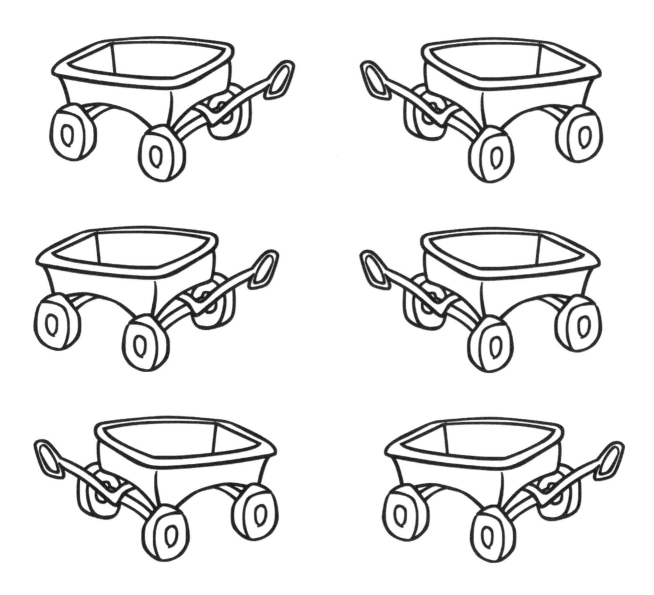

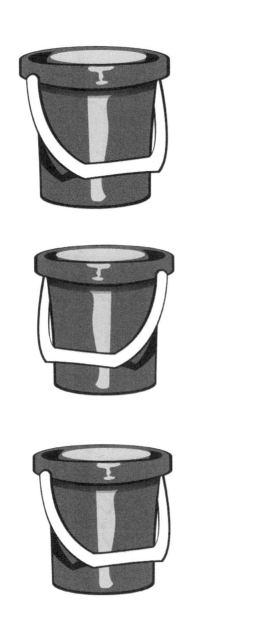

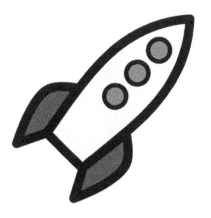

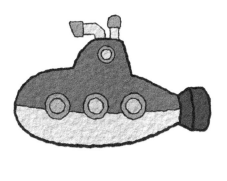

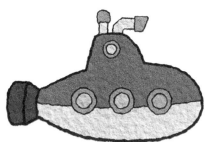

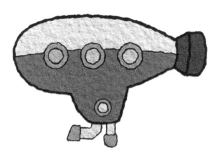

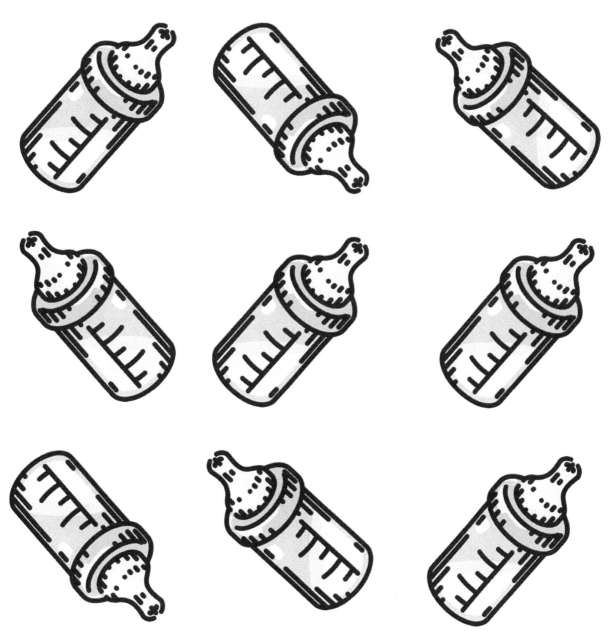

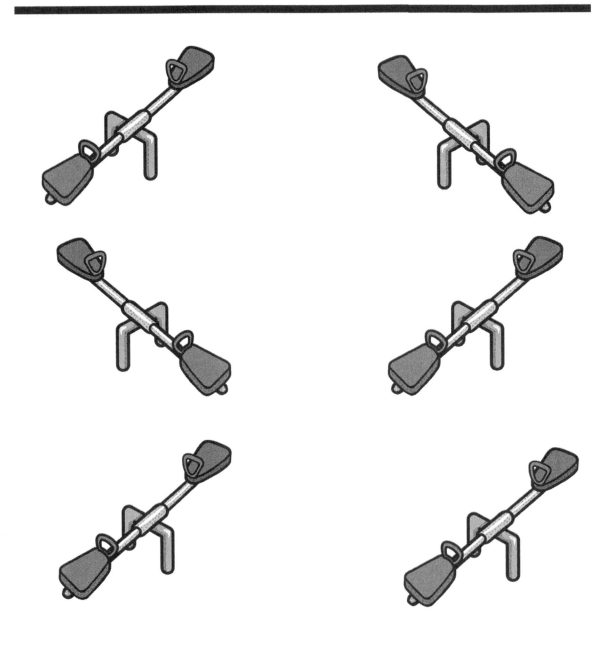

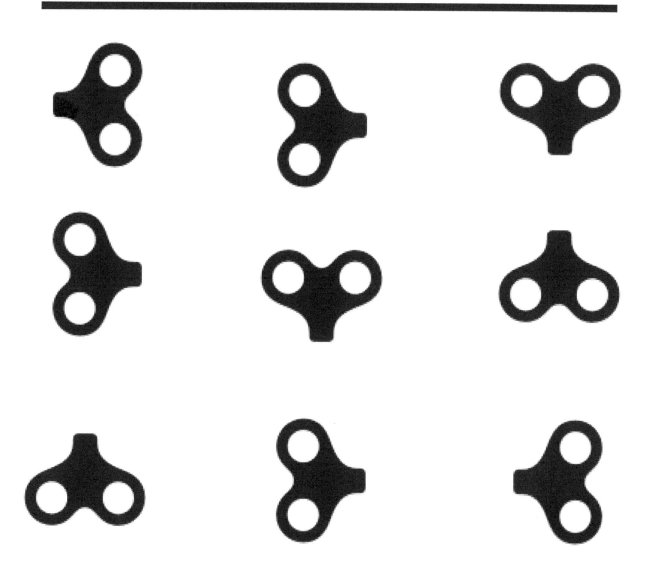

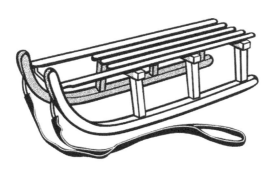

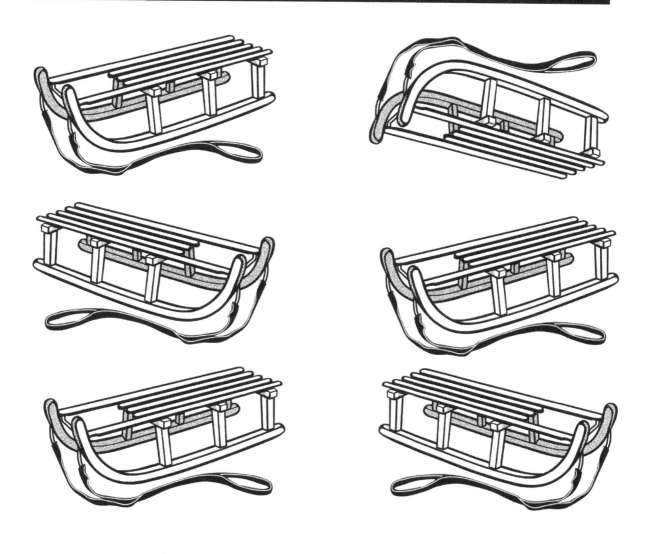

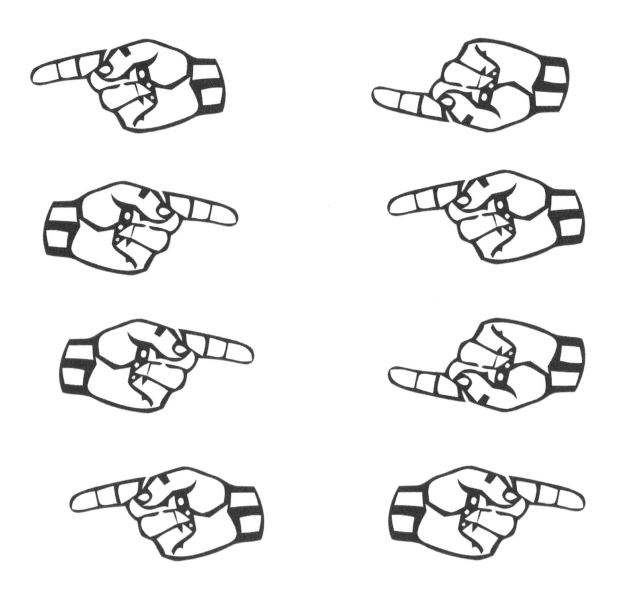

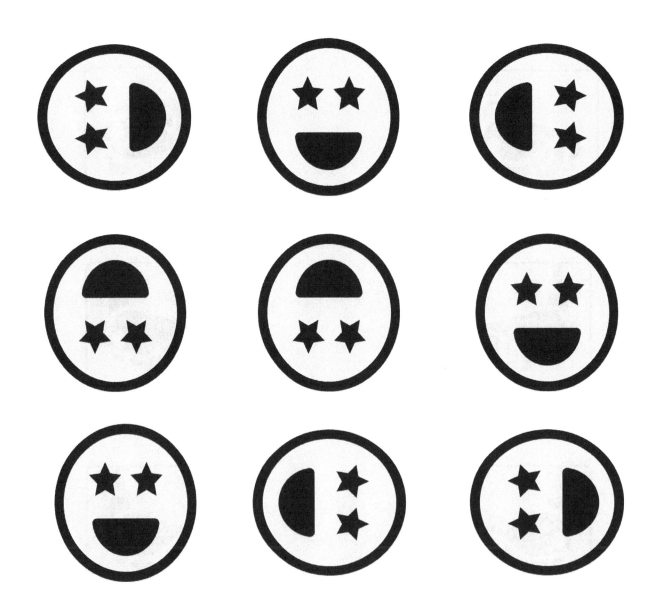

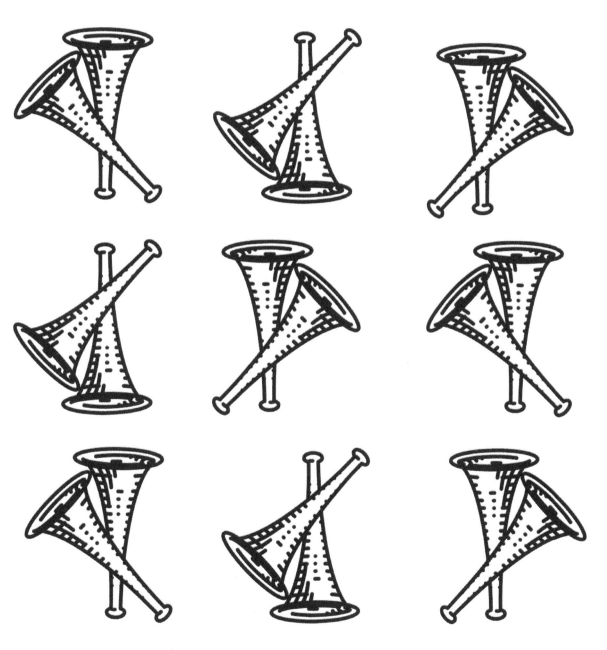

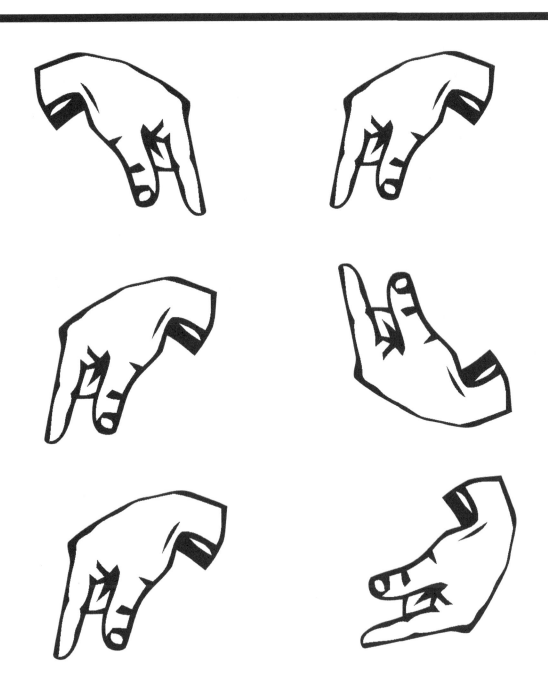

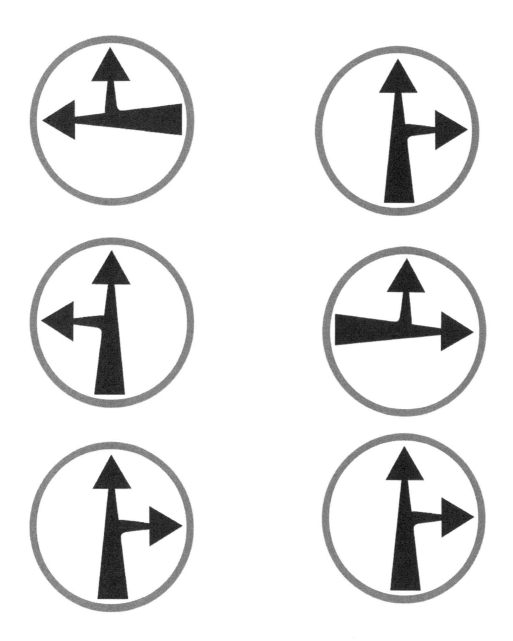

48

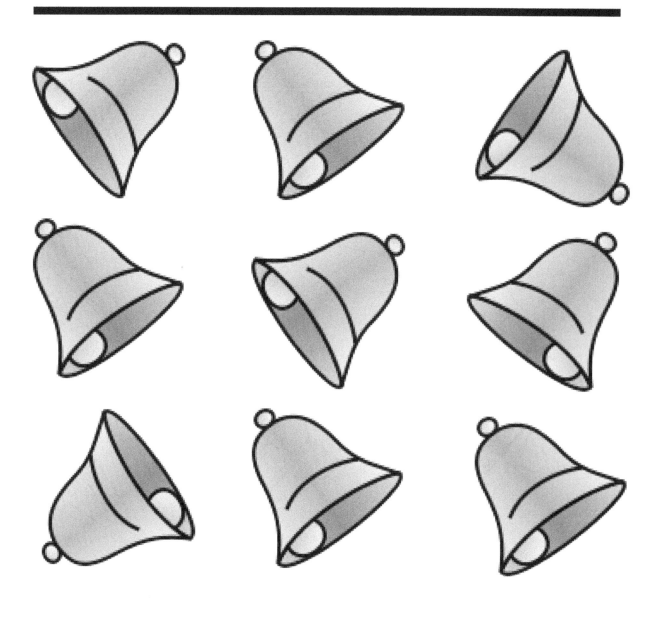

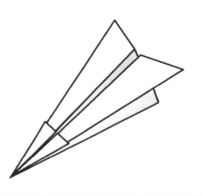

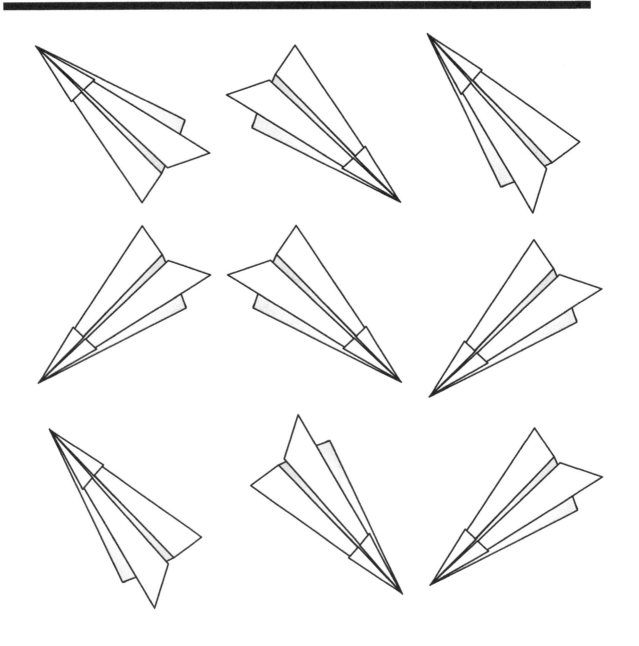

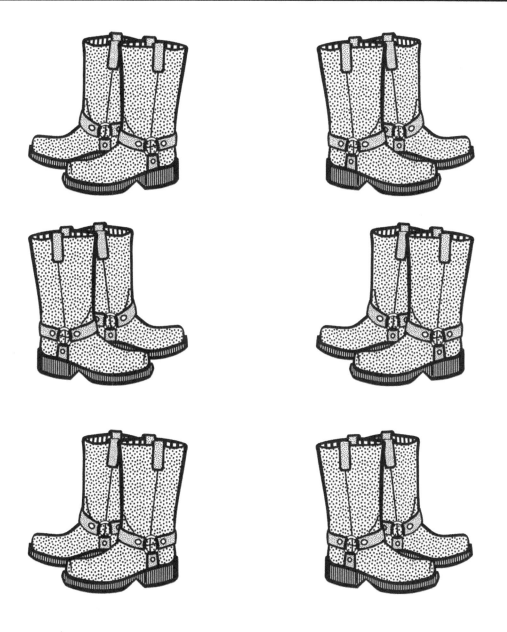

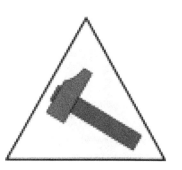

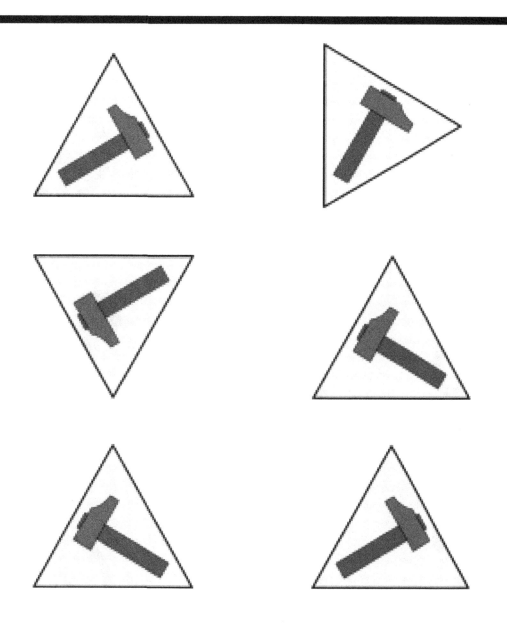

55

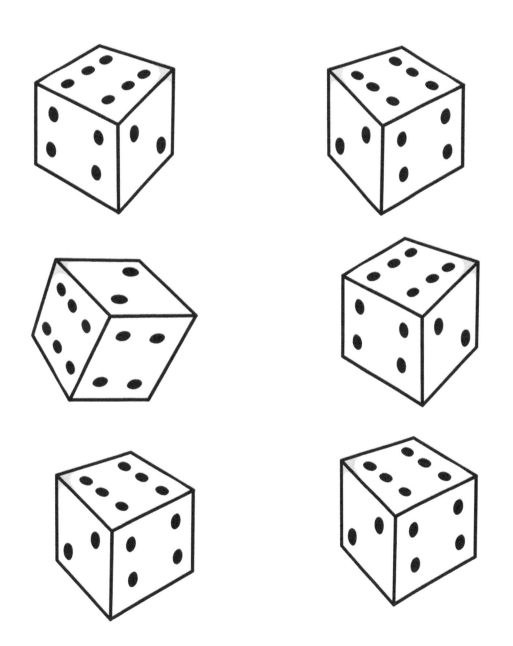

Mark the same figures as the model

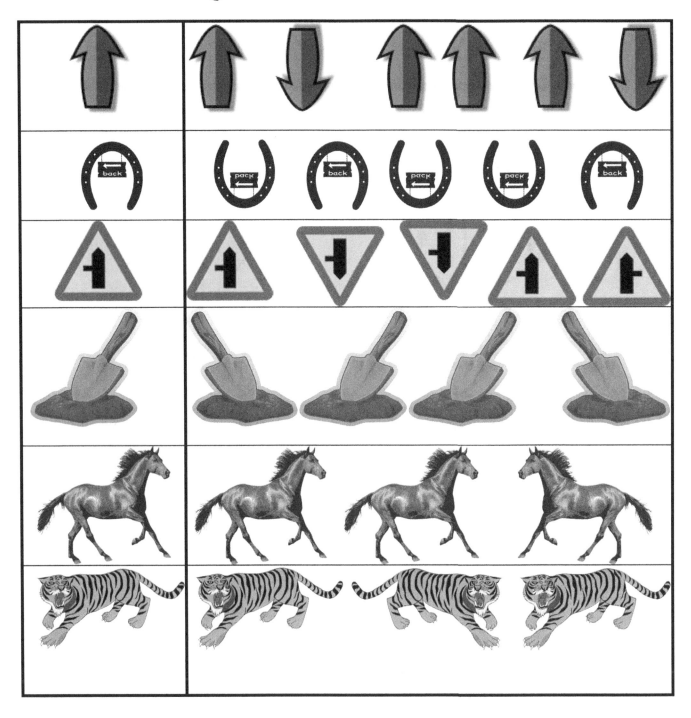

Mark the same figures as the model

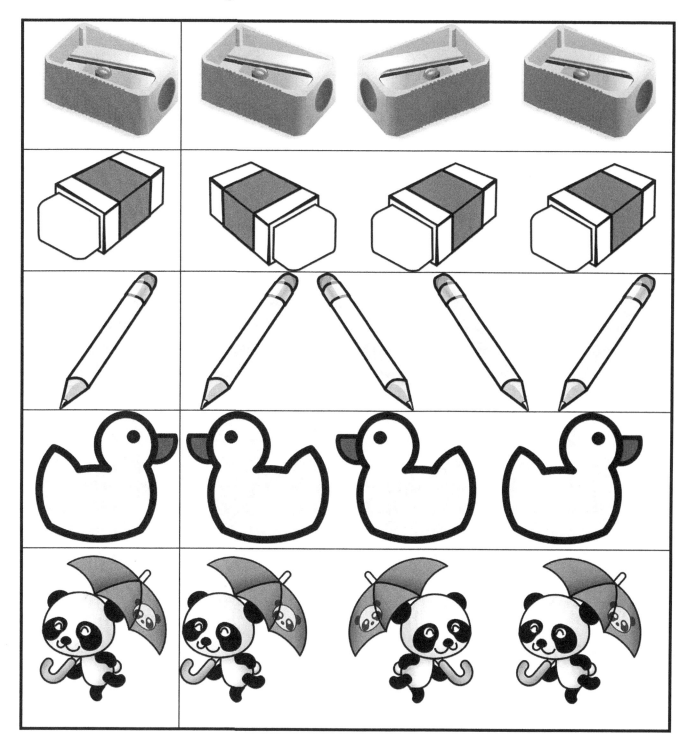

Mark the same figures as the model

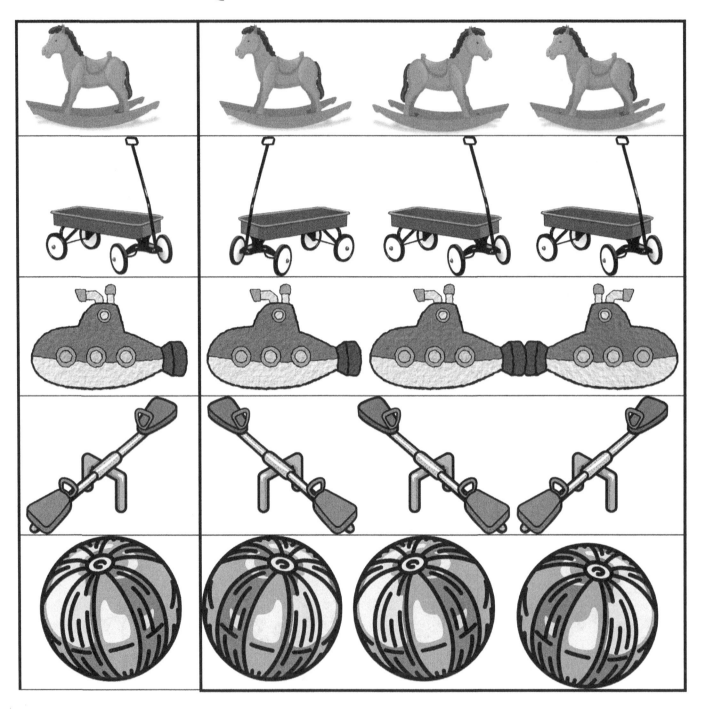

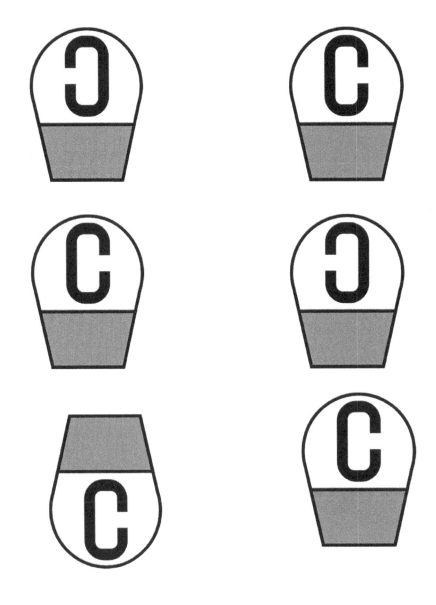

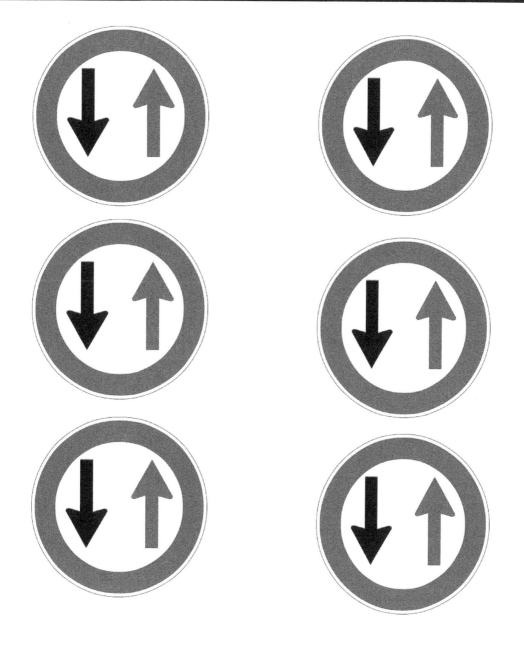

69

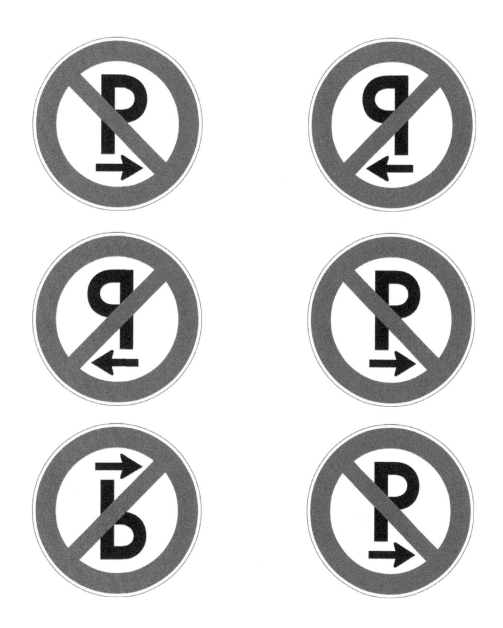

72

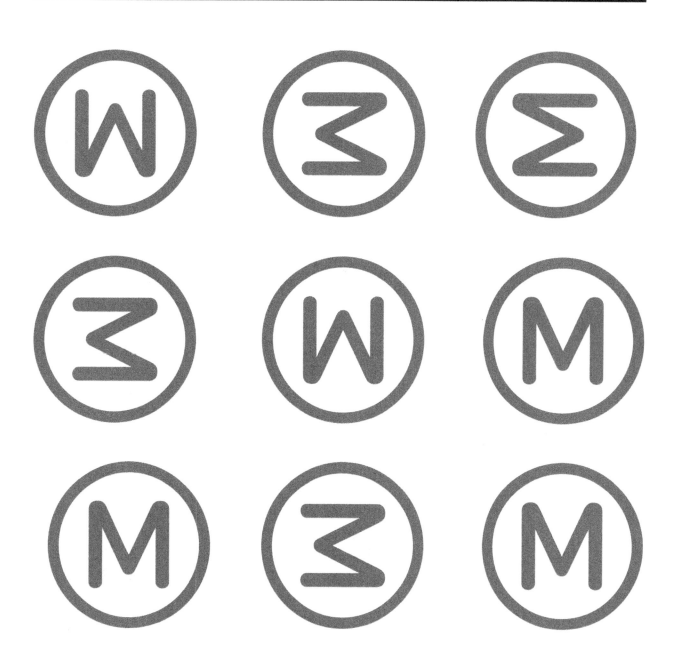

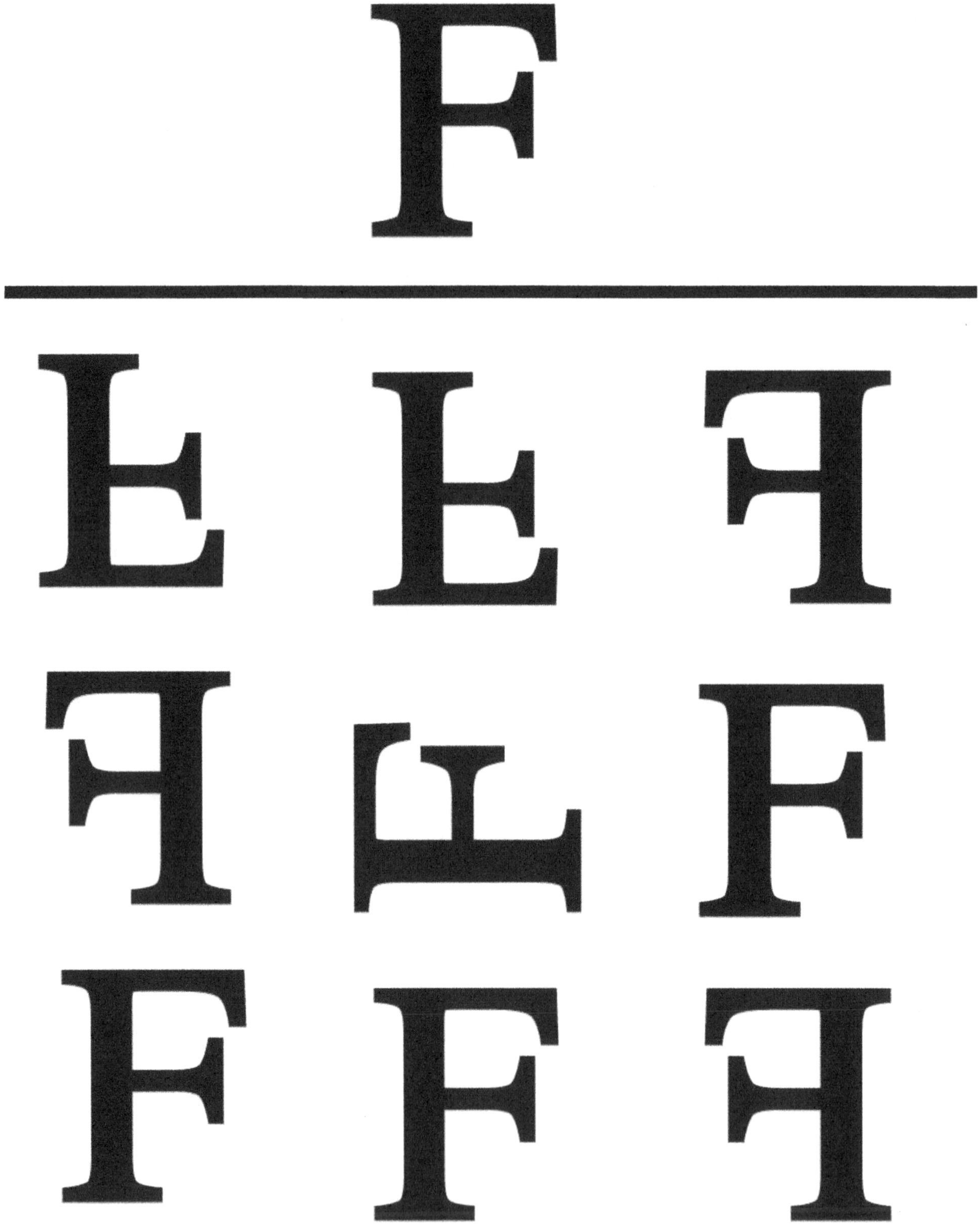

j

ï j ï ſ

j ï ? j

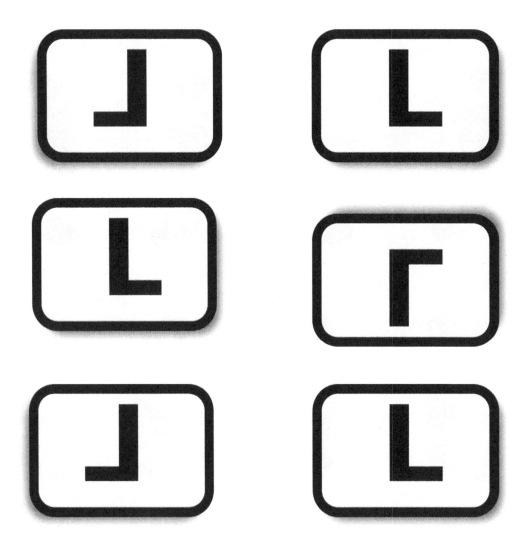

B

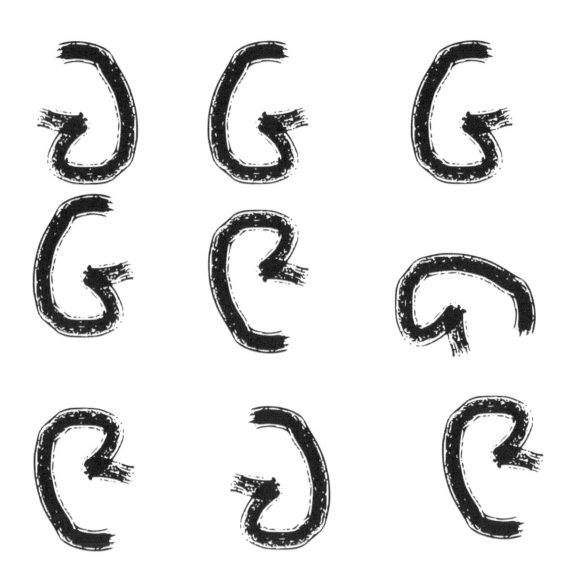

P

P d P

P P q

q P b

fb

---

fb fb dh

up dh fb

fb up dh

The author

Juan José Ibáñez Solar (Santander, ESPAÑA)

Psychologist. Accredited Psychotherapist F.E.A.P Didactic Psychoanalyst by the Association of Psychotherapists Cántabra and Master in Psychoanalytic Psychotherapy by the G.P.A.B [Analytical Psychotherapy Group. (SEPTEG, FEAP, Professional Associations, Associations and Training Groups) Pedagogue and speech therapy. He works as a counselor in early childhood, primary and secondary education centers. It performs advisory and direct intervention functions related to applied psychology in various fields, such as clinical, educational, business and training. Coordinator of the websites www.educacionpositiva.com and www.psicoanalistaonline.com

- **Other works of the author**

"Read Now!" Manual with exercises to learn to read and / or deal with reading difficulties. Contrast method. (Paperback, Spanish edition) Published on Amazon

"Dyslexia. Complete Treatment". (Paperback) Published on Amazon (English edition)

"Chemistry.Adaptation Curriculum for Secondary Education. Ebook. Spanish edition. La casa del libro (Madrid, Spain)

All works available on www.educacionpositiva.com

- **The following works (Spanish editions) are available at** www.psicoanlistaonline.com

"Basic course of psychoanalytic technique"

"Individualized orientation from a psychoanalytic perspective. Technique and cases"

"Child psychoanalysis. Technical bases and sessions."

"A sample of psychoanalytic work". Master's work. GPAB, Bilbao. Spain

"The psychoanalytic diagnosis: a practical and clear perspective."

- **Contact**

juanjose.ibanezsolar@educantabria.es

contacto@ducacionpositiva.com

This book was written in Solares, Cantabria, Spain. January 2017

Made in the USA
Middletown, DE
31 August 2023